W9-CEP-249

THE POCKET BOOK OF

hygge

THE POCKET BOOK OF

hygge

Heartwarming thoughts for
a more meaningful life

ARCTURUS

This edition published in 2017 by Arcturus Publishing Limited
26/27 Bickels Yard, 151–153 Bermondsey Street,
London SE1 3HA

ISBN: 978-1-78828-244-4
AD005971UK

Printed in China

CONTENTS

HOME

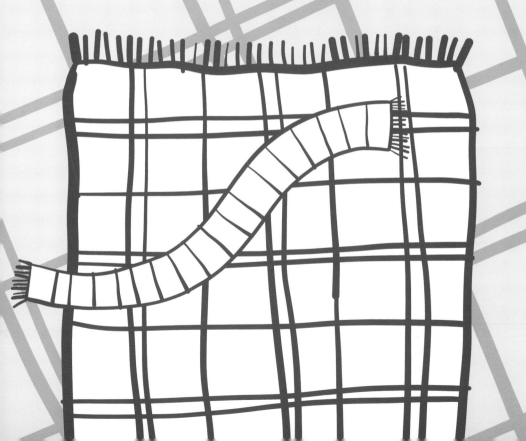

BE GRATEFUL FOR THE HOME YOU HAVE, KNOWING THAT AT THIS MOMENT, ALL YOU HAVE IS ALL YOU NEED.

Sarah Ban Breathnach

Where we love is home - home that our feet may leave, but not our hearts.

Oliver Wendell Holmes

Home is where the heart is.

Pliny the Elder

Winter is the time for comfort, for good food and warmth, for the touch of a friendly hand and for a talk beside the fire: it is the time for home.

Edith Sitwell

Where thou art, that is home.

Emily Dickinson

Home interprets heaven. Home is heaven for beginners.

Charles Henry Parkhurst

A HEART MAKES A GOOD HOME FOR THE FRIEND.

Yunus Emre

The home should be the treasure chest of living.

Le Corbusier

Any old place I can hang my hat is home sweet home to me.

William Jerome

THERE IS NOTHING MORE IMPORTANT THAN A GOOD, SAFE, SECURE HOME.

Rosalynn Carter

Seek home for rest, for home is best.

Thomas Tusser

Home is the most popular, and will be the most enduring of all earthly establishments.

Channing Pollock

When I go home, it's an easy way to be grounded. You learn to realize what truly matters.

Tony Stewart

The ache for home lives in all of us. The safe place where we can go as we are and not be questioned.

Maya Angelou

Mid pleasures and palaces though we may roam,
be it ever so humble, there's no place like home.

J. H. Payne

But every house
where love abides
and friendship is a
guest, is surely home,
and home, sweet
home, for there the
heart can rest.

Henry Van Dyke

There is nothing like staying at home for real comfort.

Jane Austen

Charity begins at home, but should not end there.

Thomas Fuller

Hospitality consists in a little fire, a little food, and an immense quiet.

Ralph Waldo Emerson

THIS DOOR WILL OPEN AT A TOUCH TO WELCOME EVERY FRIEND.

Henry Van Dyke

A man travels the world over in search of
what he needs and returns home to find it.

George Moore

A house is not a home
unless it contains food
and fire for the mind
as well as the body.

Benjamin Franklin

Is it possible for home to be a person and not a place?

Stephanie Perkins

I live in my own little world.
But it's OK, they know me here.

Lauren Myracle

It was good to walk into a library again; it smelled like home.

Elizabeth Kostova

If I ever go looking for my heart's desire again, I won't look any further than my own back yard. Because if it isn't there, I never really lost it to begin with.

L. Frank Baum

Home is the nicest word there is.

Laura Ingalls Wilder

THE ORNAMENT OF A HOUSE IS THE FRIENDS WHO FREQUENT IT.

Ralph Waldo Emerson

Home isn't a place, it's a feeling.

Cecelia Ahern

Home is everything you can walk to.

Jerry Spinelli

Home is where my habits have a habitat.

Fiona Apple

If light is in your heart, you will find your way home.

Jalaluddin Rumi

Philosophy is really nostalgia, the desire to be at home.

Novalis

I don't care if we have our house, or a cliff ledge, or a cardboard box. Home is wherever we all are, together.

James Patterson

Maybe that's the best part of going away for a vacation – coming home again.

Madeleine L'Engle

All I wanted was what I'd already had. That exultation, that love. It was my one real home; I was a visitor everywhere else.

Scott Spencer

Man wanted a home, a place for warmth, or comfort, first of physical warmth, then the warmth of the affections.

Henry David Thoreau

To me, you were more than just a person. You were a place where I finally felt at home.

Denice Envall

EVERYONE NEEDS A HOUSE TO LIVE IN, BUT A SUPPORTIVE FAMILY IS WHAT BUILDS A HOME.

Anthony Liccione

If the home is a body, the table is the heart, the beating center, the sustainer of life and health.

Shauna Niequist

Every day is a journey, and the journey itself is home.

Matsuo Bashõ

You haven't really been anywhere until you've got back home.

Terry Pratchett

What I love most about my home is who I share it with.

Tad Carpenter

YOU FEEL MORE LIKE HOME TO ME THAN ANY PLACE I'VE EVER BEEN.

Angela N. Blount

We know that when people are safe in their homes, they are free to pursue their dream for a brighter economic future for themselves and their families.

George Pataki

Home is the place where, when you have
to go there, they have to take you in.

Robert Frost

**When you finally go back to your old
home, you find it wasn't the old home
you missed but your childhood.**

Sam Ewing

I kiss the soil as if I placed a kiss on the hands of a mother, for the homeland is our earthly mother. I consider it my duty to be with my compatriots in this sublime and difficult moment.

Pope John Paul II

God is at home, it's we who have gone out for a walk.

Meister Eckhart

Think what a better world it would be if we all, the whole world, had cookies and milk about three o'clock every afternoon and then lay down on our blankets for a nap.

Barbara Jordan

I think careful cooking is love, don't you? The loveliest thing you can cook for someone who's close to you is about as nice a Valentine as you can give.

Julia Child

If you really want to make a friend, go to someone's house and eat with him... the people who give you their food give you their heart.

Cesar Chavez

Home isn't where you're from, it's where you find light when all grows dark.

Pierce Brown

If I were asked to name the chief benefit of the house, I should say: the house shelters day-dreaming, the house protects the dreamer, the house allows one to dream in peace.

Gaston Bachelard

Home is people. Not a place. If you go back there after the people are gone, then all you can see is what is not there any more.

Robin Hobb

When I eat with my friends, it is a moment of real pleasure, when I really enjoy my life.

Monica Bellucci

How often have I lain beneath rain on a strange roof, thinking of home.

William Faulkner

Nature is not a place to visit. It is home.

Gary Snyder

Every goal, every action, every thought, every feeling one experiences, whether it be consciously or unconsciously known, is an attempt to increase one's level of peace of mind.

Sydney Madwed

He that would live in peace and at ease must not speak all he knows or all he sees.

Benjamin Franklin

One does not need buildings, money, power, or status to practice the Art of Peace. Heaven is right where you are standing, and that is the place to train.

Morihei Ueshiba

To attain inner peace you must actually give your life, not just your possessions. When you at last give your life - bringing into alignment your beliefs and the way you live then, and only then, can you begin to find inner peace.

Peace Pilgrim

Peace is not an absence of war, it is a virtue, a state of mind, a disposition for benevolence, confidence, justice.

Baruch Spinoza

The simplification of life is one of the steps to inner peace. A persistent simplification will create an inner and outer well-being that places harmony in one's life.

Peace Pilgrim

Let there be work, bread, water and salt for all.

Nelson Mandela

Trust yourself. Create the kind of self that you will be happy to live with all your life. Make the most of yourself by fanning the tiny, inner sparks of possibility into flames of achievement.

Golda Meir

The most valuable possession you can own is an open heart. The most powerful weapon you can be is an instrument of peace.

Carlos Santana

Any woman who understands the problems of running a home will be nearer to understanding the problems of running a country.

Margaret Thatcher

Housework is what a woman does that nobody notices unless she hasn't done it.

Evan Esar

Decorate your home. It gives the illusion that your life is more interesting than it really is.

Charles M. Schulz

HOME WASN'T BUILT IN A DAY.

Jane Sherwood Ace

I'm the type who'd be happy not going anywhere as long as I was sure I knew exactly what was happening at the places I wasn't going to. I'm the type who'd like to sit home and watch every party that I'm invited to on a monitor in my bedroom.

Andy Warhol

You never know what events are
going to transpire to get you home.

Og Mandino

I DO NOT RECALL A JEWISH HOME WITHOUT A BOOK ON THE TABLE.

Elie Wiesel

In our home there was always prayer – aloud, proud and unapologetic.

Lyndon B. Johnson

Home is any four walls that enclose the right person.

Helen Rowland

I feel like I've never had a home, you know? I feel related to the country, to this country, and yet I don't know exactly where I fit in... There's always this kind of nostalgia for a place, a place where you can reckon with yourself.

Sam Shepard

Never make your home in a place.
Make a home for yourself inside
your own head. You'll find what you
need to furnish it – memory, friends
you can trust, love of learning, and
other such things. That way it will
go with you wherever you journey.

Tad Williams

A MAN'S HOME IS HIS WIFE'S CASTLE.

Alexander Chase

If your house is burning, wouldn't you try and put out the fire?

Imran Khan

I love grocery shopping when I'm home. That's what makes me feel totally normal. I love both the idea of home as in being with my family and friends, and also the idea of exploration. I think those two are probably my great interests.

Yo-Yo Ma

The home is the chief school of human virtues.

William Ellery Channing

Home is one's birthplace, ratified by memory.

Henry Anatole Grunwald

Homesickness is nothing. Fifty percent of the people in the world are homesick all the time.

John Cheever

I am not quite sure where home is right now. I do have places in London and Milan, and a house in Spain. I guess I would say home is where my mother is.

Sarah Brightman

The fellow that owns his own home is always just coming out of a hardware store.

Kin Hubbard

KINDNESS GOES A LONG WAYS LOTS OF TIMES WHEN IT OUGHT TO STAY AT HOME.

Kin Hubbard

There are only two things we should fight for. One is the defense of our homes and the other is the Bill of Rights.

Smedley Butler

I'm lucky because I have a job I love. I really miss being away from home, being in my own bed, seeing my animals and siblings, having my mom's cookies. I have a couple cats. I got a kitten about a year ago and now I'm going on the road so I won't see him for a while. I feel bad.

Michelle Branch

HOME IS THE PLACE WE LOVE BEST AND GRUMBLE THE MOST.

Billy Sunday

There is something permanent, and something extremely profound, in owning a home.

Kenny Guinn

Since I travel so much, it's always great to be home. There's nothing like getting to raid my own refrigerator at two in the morning.

Amy Grant

I grew up in a household where everybody lived at the top of his lungs.

Frank Langella

The home to everyone is to him his castle and fortress, as well for his defence against injury and violence, as for his repose.

Edward Coke

IT TAKES A HEAP O' LIVIN' IN A HOUSE T' MAKE IT A HOME.

Edgar A. Guest

Does anybody mind if I don't live in a house that is quaint? Because, for one thing, quaint houses are generally houses where plumbing ain't.

Ogden Nash

A comfortable house is a great source of happiness. It ranks immediately after health and a good conscience.

Sydney Smith

The house has to please everyone, contrary to the work of art, which does not. The work is a private matter for the artist. The house is not.

Adolf Loos

A MAN'S HOUSE IS HIS CASTLE.

James Otis

Run a home like you would a small business and treat it with the same seriousness.

Anthea Turner

I say, if everybody in this house lives where it's God first, friends and family second and you third, we won't ever have an argument.

Jeff Foxworthy

THE PROSPECT OF GOING HOME IS VERY APPEALING.

David Ginola

To be a queen of a household is a powerful thing.

Jill Scott

People who have good relationships at home are more effective in the marketplace.

Zig Ziglar

Home, nowadays, is a place where part of the family waits till the rest of the family brings the car back.

Earl Wilson

Love begins at home, and it is not how much we do... but how much love we put in that action.

Mother Teresa

I'M GOING TO BUY SOME GREEN BANANAS BECAUSE BY THE TIME I GET HOME THEY'LL BE RIPE.

Ryan Stiles

TIME AND PLACE

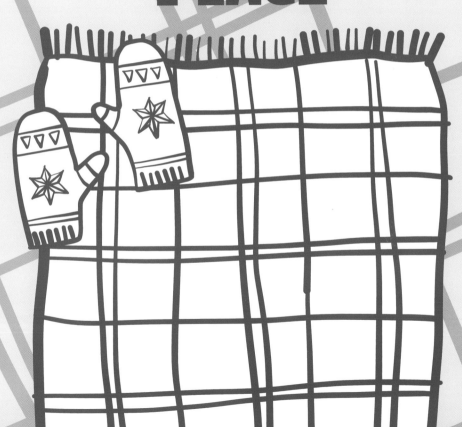

Life is full of beauty.
Notice it. Notice the
bumblebee, the small
child, and the smiling
faces. Smell the rain,
and feel the wind.
Live your life to the
fullest potential, and
fight for your dreams.

Ashley Smith

Everyone can identify with a fragrant garden, with beauty of sunset, with the quiet of nature, with a warm and cosy cottage.

Thomas Kincade

A thing of beauty is a joy forever: its loveliness increases: it will never pass into nothingness.

John Keats

EVERYTHING HAS BEAUTY, BUT NOT EVERYONE SEES IT.

Confucius

The only thing that ultimately matters is to eat an ice-cream cone, play a slide trombone, plant a small tree: good God, now you're free.

Ray Manzarek

The pursuit of truth and beauty
is a sphere of activity in which
we are permitted to remain
children all our lives.

Albert Einstein

Never lose an
opportunity of seeing
anything beautiful,
for beauty is God's
handwriting.

Ralph Waldo Emerson

Don't judge each day by the harvest you reap but by the seeds that you plant.

Robert Louis Stevenson

How goodness heightens beauty!

Milan Kundera

Beauty is the promise of happiness.

Edmund Burke

LET US LIVE FOR THE BEAUTY OF OUR OWN REALITY.

Charles Lamb

RARE IS THE UNION OF BEAUTY AND PURITY.

Juvenal

Always bear in mind that your own resolution to succeed is more important than any other.

Abraham Lincoln

We live in a wonderful world that is full of beauty, charm and adventure. There is no end to the adventures that we can have if only we seek them with our eyes open.

Jawaharlal Nehru

Once upon a time there was a piece of wood. It was not an expensive piece of wood. Far from it. Just a common block of firewood, one of those thick, solid logs that are put on the fire in winter to make cold rooms cosy and warm.

Carlo Collodi

73

IT'S THE BEST FEELING WHEN YOU WAKE UP AND IT'S WARM AND COSY, AND YOU DON'T HAVE TO GO TO WORK.

Emmy Rossum

I like to go out, but sometimes it's nice to stay cosy at home, watching movies or TV, especially early in the week.

Charlotte Ronson

Did I offer peace today? Did I bring a smile to someone's face? Did I say words of healing? Did I let go of my anger and resentment? Did I forgive? Did I love? These are the real questions. I must trust that the little bit of love that I sow now will bear many fruits, here in this world and the life to come.

Henri Nouwen

She craved a tall glass of the fresh-squeezed lemonade from the pitcher she'd left chilling in the fridge. Two glasses served with a generous slice of pound cake with orange glaze icing sounded twice as nice.

Ed Lynskey

There's nothing as cozy as a piece of candy and a book.

Betty MacDonald

All day the storm lasted. The windows were white and the wind never stopped howling and screaming. It was pleasant in the warm house. Laura and Mary did their lessons, then Pa played the fiddle while Ma rocked and knitted, and bean soup simmered on the stove. All night the storm lasted, and all the next day. Fire-light danced out of the stove's draught, and Pa told stories and played the fiddle.

Laura Ingalls Wilder

Having her favorite breakfast always made her feel cosy, like a warm blanket was being wrapped around her.

Jessica Haight and Stephanie Robinson

Rain is sexy. I like rain. But the car will be cosy. I like cosy things more. And I like the things that make me cosy.

Ritika Chhabra

SOUP IS COSY.

A. D. Posey

I often think that the night is more alive and more richly coloured than the day.

Vincent Van Gogh

The joy of life comes from our encounters with new experiences, and hence there is no greater joy than to have an endlessly changing horizon, for each day to have a new and different sun.

Christopher McCandless

You have to enjoy life.
Always be surrounded
by people that you like,
people who have a nice
conversation. There are
so many positive things
to think about.

Sophia Loren

Look up, laugh loud, talk big, keep the colour in your cheek and the fire in your eye, adorn your person, maintain your health, your beauty and your animal spirits.

William Hazlitt

I truly believe that everything that we do and everyone that we meet is put in our path for a purpose. There are no accidents; we're all teachers – if we're willing to pay attention to the lessons we learn, trust our positive instincts and not be afraid to take risks or wait for some miracle to come knocking at our door.

Marla Gibbs

POSITIVE THINKING WILL LET YOU USE THE ABILITY WHICH YOU HAVE, AND THAT IS AWESOME.

Zig Ziglar

I can't live without my beauty products. I love to be in my bathroom with my candles lit, morning, noon and night. I like taking hot baths and hot showers, using my body scrubs and lotions.

Traci Bingham

Real beauty is to be true to oneself. That's what makes me feel good.

Laetitia Casta

DON'T AIM FOR SUCCESS IF YOU WANT IT; JUST DO WHAT YOU LOVE AND BELIEVE IN, AND IT WILL COME NATURALLY.

David Frost

When what we are is what we want to be,
that's happiness.

Malcolm Forbes

Happiness grows at
our own firesides, and
is not to be picked in
strangers' gardens.

Douglas William Jerrold

Be as smart as you can,
but remember that it is
always better to be wise
than to be smart.

Alan Alda

Success is getting what you want. Happiness is wanting what you get.

Dale Carnegie

You must try to generate happiness within yourself. If you aren't happy in one place, chances are you won't be happy anyplace.

Ernie Banks

MAN BECOMES MAN ONLY BY HIS INTELLIGENCE, BUT HE IS MAN ONLY BY HIS HEART.

Henri Frederic Amiel

The mind is not
a vessel to be
filled but a fire
to be kindled.

Plutarch

If you wait for the perfect moment when
all is safe and assured, it may never arrive.
Mountains will not be climbed, races won,
or lasting happiness achieved.

Maurice Chevalier

THERE IS ONLY ONE SUCCESS - TO BE ABLE TO SPEND YOUR LIFE IN YOUR OWN WAY.

Christopher Morley

Good management is the art of making problems so interesting and their solutions so constructive that everyone wants to get to work and deal with them.

Paul Hawken

Getting in touch with your true self must be your first priority.

Tom Hopkins

HOLD YOURSELF RESPONSIBLE FOR A HIGHER STANDARD THAN ANYBODY EXPECTS OF YOU. NEVER EXCUSE YOURSELF.

Henry Ward Beecher

You change your life by changing your heart.

Max Lucado

CLIMB THE MOUNTAINS AND GET THEIR GOOD TIDINGS.

John Muir

I HAVE LOOKED INTO YOUR EYES WITH MY EYES. I HAVE PUT MY HEART NEAR YOUR HEART.

Pope John XXIII

Don't follow any advice, no matter how good, until you feel as deeply in your spirit as you think in your mind that the counsel is wise.

Joan Rivers

CLOUDS COME FLOATING INTO MY LIFE, NO LONGER TO CARRY RAIN OR USHER STORM, BUT TO ADD COLOUR TO MY SUNSET SKY.

Rabindranath Tagore

By three methods we may learn wisdom: First, by reflection, which is noblest; second, by imitation, which is easiest; and third by experience, which is the bitterest.

Confucius

Just what future the Designer of the universe has provided for the souls of men I do not know, I cannot prove. But I find that the whole order of Nature confirms my confidence that, if it is not like our noblest hopes and dreams, it will transcend them.

Henry Norris Russell

WISDOM, COMPASSION, AND COURAGE ARE THE THREE UNIVERSALLY RECOGNIZED MORAL QUALITIES OF MEN.

Confucius

Wonder rather than doubt is the root of all knowledge.

Abraham Joshua Heschel

WISDOM BEGINS IN WONDER.

Socrates

TEARS OF JOY ARE LIKE THE SUMMER RAIN DROPS PIERCED BY SUNBEAMS.

Hosea Ballou

Nothing makes one feel so strong as a call for help.

Pope Paul VI

Thought is the wind, knowledge the sail, and mankind the vessel.

Augustus Hare

Life is 10 percent
what you make
it, and 90 percent
how you take it.

Irving Berlin

To love beauty
is to see light.

Victor Hugo

I HAVE A SIMPLE PHILOSOPHY: FILL WHAT'S EMPTY. EMPTY WHAT'S FULL. SCRATCH WHERE IT ITCHES.

Alice Roosevelt Longworth

All the art of living lies in a fine mingling of letting go and holding on.

Havelock Ellis

Be what you are. This is the first step toward becoming better than you are.

Julius Charles Hare

GO CONFIDENTLY IN THE DIRECTION OF YOUR DREAMS. LIVE THE LIFE YOU HAVE IMAGINED.

Henry David Thoreau

It's better to be a lion for a day than a sheep all your life.

Elizabeth Kenny

Don't go through life, grow through life.

Eric Butterworth

LIFE CONSISTS NOT IN HOLDING GOOD CARDS BUT IN PLAYING THOSE YOU HOLD WELL.

Josh Billings

To be satisfied with a little, is the greatest wisdom; and he that increaseth his riches, increaseth his cares; but a contented mind is a hidden treasure, and trouble findeth it not.

Akhenaten

We must be willing to let go of the life we have planned, so as to have the life that is waiting for us.

E. M. Forster

Good friends, good books and a sleepy conscience: this is the ideal life.

Mark Twain

IT TAKES A GREAT MAN TO GIVE SOUND ADVICE TACTFULLY, BUT A GREATER TO ACCEPT IT GRACIOUSLY.

Logan P. Smith

Be happy. It's one way of being wise.

Sidonie Gabrielle Colette

Good nature is worth more than knowledge, more than money, more than honor, to the persons who possess it.

Henry Ward Beecher

Our life is what our thoughts make it.

Marcus Aurelius

I have found that if you love life, life will love you back.

Arthur Rubinstein

In this world
it is not what
we take up, but
what we give
up, that makes
us rich.

Henry Ward Beecher

I believe the only thing that we really have
control over is our attitude. If we focus on the
positive things in our lives and learn how to cope
with all the surprises, we will be happier people.

Brandon Jenner

AN AIM IN LIFE IS THE ONLY FORTUNE WORTH FINDING.

Robert Louis Stevenson

Not life, but good life, is to be chiefly valued.

Socrates

Life is far too important a thing ever to talk seriously about.

Oscar Wilde

I TAKE CARE OF MY FLOWERS AND MY CATS. AND ENJOY FOOD. AND THAT'S LIVING.

Ursula Andress

Opportunity does not knock, it presents itself when you beat down the door.

Kyle Chandler

There is just one life for each of us: our own.

Euripides

What you do today can improve all your tomorrows.

Ralph Marston

To me, a building – if it's beautiful – is the love of one man, he's made it out of his love for space, materials, things like that.

Martha Graham

Small deeds done are better than great deeds planned.

Peter Marshall

Do not dwell in the past, do not dream of the future, concentrate the mind on the present moment.

Buddha

SETTING GOALS IS THE FIRST STEP IN TURNING THE INVISIBLE INTO THE VISIBLE.

Tony Robbins

Simplicity is the ultimate sophistication.

Leonardo da Vinci

The greatest wealth is to live content with little.

Plato

Nevertheless, whether in occurrences lasting days, hours or mere minutes at a time, I have experienced happiness often, and have had brief encounters with it in my later years, even in old age.

Herman Hesse

I FELT MY LUNGS INFLATE WITH THE ONRUSH OF SCENERY - AIR, MOUNTAINS, TREES, PEOPLE. I THOUGHT, 'THIS IS WHAT IT IS TO BE HAPPY.'

Sylvia Plath

Those who contemplate the beauty of the earth find reserves of strength that will endure as long as life lasts. ... There is something infinitely healing in the repeated refrains of nature – the assurance that dawn comes after night, and spring after winter.

Rachel Carson

We shape our buildings; thereafter they shape us.

Winston Churchill

These people have learned not from books, but in the fields, in the wood, on the river bank. Their teachers have been the birds themselves, when they sang to them, the sun when it left a glow of crimson behind it at setting, the very trees, and wild herbs.

Anton Chekhov

WHATEVER GOOD THINGS WE BUILD END UP BUILDING US.

Jim Rohn

Miracles occur naturally as expressions of love. The real miracle is the love that inspires them. In this sense everything that comes from love is a miracle.

Marianne Williamson

FULFILLING FRIENDSHIP

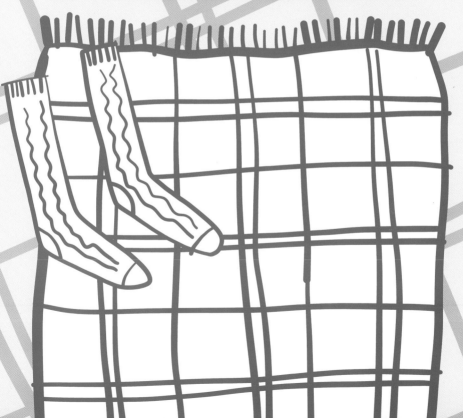

A single rose can be my garden... a single friend, my world.

Leo Buscaglia

Let us be grateful to people who make us happy, they are the charming gardeners who make our souls blossom.

Marcel Proust

FRIENDSHIP IS A SINGLE SOUL DWELLING IN TWO BODIES.

Aristotle

Friends show their love in times of trouble.

Euripides

Friendship is one mind in two bodies.

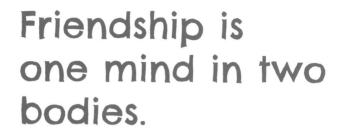

Mencius

Nothing but heaven itself is better than a friend who is really a friend.

Plautus

A friend should be one in whose understanding and virtue we can equally confide, and whose opinion we can value at once for its justness and its sincerity.

Robert Hall

THE MOST I CAN DO FOR MY FRIEND IS SIMPLY BE HIS FRIEND.

Henry David Thoreau

It's easy to impress me. I don't need a fancy party to be happy. Just good friends, good food and good laughs. I'm happy. I'm satisfied. I'm content.

Maria Sharapova

The friend who can be silent with us in a moment of despair or confusion, who can stay with us in an hour of grief and bereavement, who can tolerate not knowing... not healing, not curing... that is a friend who cares.

Henri Nouwen

It is not so much our friends' help that helps us, as the confidence of their help.

Epicurus

Lots of people want to ride with you in the limo, but what you want is someone who will take the bus with you when the limo breaks down.

Oprah Winfrey

There is nothing I would not do for those who are really my friends. I have no notion of loving people by halves, it is not my nature.

Jane Austen

If I had a flower for every time I thought of you ... I could walk through my garden forever.

Alfred Tennyson

When someone loves you, the way they talk about you is different. You feel safe and comfortable.

Jess C. Scott

THERE IS NOTHING BETTER THAN A FRIEND, UNLESS IT IS A FRIEND WITH CHOCOLATE.

Linda Grayson

I would rather walk with a friend in the dark, than alone in the light.

Helen Keller

You are my best friend as well as my lover, and I do not know which side of you I enjoy the most. I treasure each side, just as I have treasured our life together.

Nicholas Sparks

If you have two friends in your lifetime, you're lucky. If you have one good friend, you're more than lucky.

S.E. Hinton

Silence makes the real conversations between friends. Not the saying, but the never needing to say that counts.

Margaret Lee Runbeck

The glory of friendship is not the outstretched hand, not the kindly smile, nor the joy of companionship; it is the spiritual inspiration that comes to one when you discover that someone else believes in you and is willing to trust you with a friendship.

Ralph Waldo Emerson

Friendship marks a life even more deeply than love. Love risks degenerating into obsession, friendship is never anything but sharing.

Elie Wiesel

Never leave a friend behind.
Friends are all we have to get us
through this life – and they are the
only things from this world that we
could hope to see in the next.

Dean Koontz

The friend who holds your hand and
says the wrong thing is made of dearer
stuff than the one who stays away.

Barbara Kingsolver

THERE'S NOT A WORD YET, FOR OLD FRIENDS WHO'VE JUST MET.

Jim Henson

There is no exercise better for the heart than reaching down and lifting people up.

John Holmes

THE PAIN OF PARTING IS NOTHING TO THE JOY OF MEETING AGAIN.

Charles Dickens

Your friends will know you better in the first minute you meet than your acquaintances will know you in a thousand years.

Richard Bach

A friend may be waiting behind a stranger's face.

Maya Angelou

No human relation gives one possession in another – every two souls are absolutely different. In friendship or in love, the two side by side raise hands together to find what one cannot reach alone.

Kahlil Gibran

A hug is like a boomerang - you get it back right away.

Bil Keane

Be courteous to all, but intimate with few, and let those few be well tried before you give them your confidence.

George Washington

Don't walk behind me; I may not lead.
Don't walk in front of me; I may not follow.
Just walk beside me and be my friend.

Albert Camus

In everyone's life, at some time, our inner
fire goes out. It is then burst into flame by
an encounter with another human being.
We should all be thankful for those people
who rekindle the inner spirit.

Albert Schweitzer

**But friendship is precious, not only in
the shade, but in the sunshine of life, and
thanks to a benevolent arrangement the
greater part of life is sunshine.**

Thomas Jefferson

We call that person who has lost his father, an orphan; and a widower that man who has lost his wife. But that man who has known the immense unhappiness of losing a friend, by what name do we call him? Here every language is silent and holds its peace in impotence.

Joseph Roux

A true friend never gets in your way
unless you happen to be going down.

Arnold H. Glasow

A CREATIVE MAN IS MOTIVATED BY THE DESIRE TO ACHIEVE, NOT BY THE DESIRE TO BEAT OTHERS.

Ayn Rand

Always do your best. What you plant now, you will harvest later.

Og Mandino

If you can dream it, you can do it.

Walt Disney

Determine never to be idle. No person will have occasion to complain of the want of time who never loses any. It is wonderful how much may be done if we are always doing.

Thomas Jefferson

Act as if what you do makes a difference. It does.

William James

A friend is one who knows you and loves you just the same.

Elbert Hubbard

I DON'T BELIEVE YOU HAVE TO BE BETTER THAN EVERYBODY ELSE. I BELIEVE YOU HAVE TO BE BETTER THAN YOU EVER THOUGHT YOU COULD BE.

Ken Venturi

Do you want to know who you are? Don't ask. Act! Action will delineate and define you.

Thomas Jefferson

When we honestly ask ourselves which person in our lives means the most to us, we often find that it is those who, instead of giving advice, solutions, or cures, have chosen rather to share our pain and touch our wounds with a warm and tender hand.

Henri Nouwen

A friendship can weather most things and thrive in thin soil; but it needs a little mulch of letters and phone calls and small, silly presents every so often – just to save it from drying out completely.

Pam Brown

Think where man's glory most begins and ends, and say my glory was I had such friends.

William Butler Yeats

Follow your dreams, work hard, practice and persevere. Make sure you eat a variety of foods, get plenty of exercise and maintain a healthy lifestyle.

Sasha Cohen

Be gentle to all and stern with yourself.

Saint Teresa of Avila

Friendship... is not something you learn in school. But if you haven't learned the meaning of friendship, you really haven't learned anything.

Muhammad Ali

I HAVE FRIENDS IN OVERALLS WHOSE FRIENDSHIP I WOULD NOT SWAP FOR THE FAVOR OF THE KINGS OF THE WORLD.

Thomas A. Edison

But friendship is the breathing rose,
with sweets in every fold.

Oliver Wendell Holmes

If instead of a gem,
or even a flower, we
should cast the gift of
a loving thought into
the heart of a friend,
that would be giving
as the angels give.

George MacDonald

157

I always felt that the great high privilege, relief and comfort of friendship was that one had to explain nothing.

Katherine Mansfield

The key is to keep company only with people who uplift you, whose presence calls forth your best.

Epictetus

In motivating people, you've got to engage their minds and their hearts. I motivate people, I hope, by example – and perhaps by excitement, by having productive ideas to make others feel involved.

Rupert Murdoch

One's friends are that part of the human race with which one can be human.

George Santayana

I value the friend who for me finds time on his calendar, but I cherish the friend who for me does not consult his calendar.

Robert Brault

The more man meditates upon good thoughts,
the better will be his world and the world at large.

Confucius

Friends and good
manners will carry you
where money won't go.

Margaret Walker

A FRIENDSHIP FOUNDED ON BUSINESS IS BETTER THAN A BUSINESS FOUNDED ON FRIENDSHIP.

John D. Rockefeller

To be a good loser is
to learn how to win.

Carl Sandburg

**Being deeply loved by
someone gives you
strength, while loving
someone deeply gives
you courage.**

Lao Tzu

What is called genius
is the abundance of
life and health.

Henry David Thoreau

Can miles truly separate you from friends... If you want to be with someone you love, aren't you already there?

Richard Bach

Let us always meet each other with a smile, for the smile is the beginning of love.

Mother Teresa

A part of kindness consists in loving people more than they deserve.

Joseph Joubert

If you live to be a hundred, I want to live to be a hundred minus one day so I never have to live without you.

A. A. Milne

Friendship often ends in love;
but love in friendship - never.

Charles Caleb Colton

I WAS BORN WITH AN ENORMOUS NEED FOR AFFECTION, AND A TERRIBLE NEED TO GIVE IT.

Audrey Hepburn

Love is a force more formidable than any other. It is invisible – it cannot be seen or measured, yet it is powerful enough to transform you in a moment, and offer you more joy than any material possession could.

Barbara de Angelis

Love yourself first and everything else falls into line. You really have to love yourself to get anything done in this world.

Lucille Ball

Don't brood. Get on with living and loving. You don't have forever.

Leo Buscaglia

We are not the same persons this year as last; nor are those we love. It is a happy chance if we, changing, continue to love a changed person.

W. Somerset Maugham

I DON'T NEED A FRIEND WHO CHANGES WHEN I CHANGE AND WHO NODS WHEN I NOD; MY SHADOW DOES THAT MUCH BETTER.

Plutarch

Friends
are born,
not made.

Henry B. Adams

TRUE FRIENDS STAB YOU IN THE FRONT.

Oscar Wilde

A loving heart is the truest wisdom.

Charles Dickens

Men kick friendship around like a football, but it doesn't seem to crack. Women treat it like glass and it goes to pieces.

Anne Morrow Lindbergh

If it's very painful for you to criticize your friends – you're safe in doing it. But if you take the slightest pleasure in it, that's the time to hold your tongue.

Alice Duer Miller

Never explain - your friends do not need it and your enemies will not believe you anyway.

Elbert Hubbard

IT IS ONE OF THE BLESSINGS OF OLD FRIENDS THAT YOU CAN AFFORD TO BE STUPID WITH THEM.

Ralph Waldo Emerson

Fear makes strangers of people who would be friends.

Shirley MacLaine

You can always tell a real friend: when you've made a fool of yourself he doesn't feel you've done a permanent job.

Laurence J. Peter

It's the friends you can call up at 4 a.m. that matter.

Marlene Dietrich

Friendship is held to be the severest test of character. It is easy, we think, to be loyal to a family and clan, whose blood is in your own veins.

Charles Alexander Eastman

When you choose your friends, don't be short-changed by choosing personality over character.

W. Somerset Maugham

She is a friend of mind. She gather me, man. The pieces I am, she gather them and give them back to me in all the right order. It's good, you know, when you got a woman who is a friend of your mind.

Toni Morrison

When a friend is in trouble, don't annoy him by asking if there is anything you can do. Think up something appropriate and do it.

Edward W. Howe

It takes a long time to grow an old friend.

John Leonard

Friendship needs no words - it is solitude delivered from the anguish of loneliness.

Dag Hammarskjold

The language of friendship is not words but meanings.

Henry David Thoreau

A man's growth is seen in the successive choirs of his friends.

Ralph Waldo Emerson

THE SINCERE FRIENDS OF THIS WORLD ARE AS SHIP LIGHTS IN THE STORMIEST OF NIGHTS.

Giotto di Bondone

The friend is the man who knows
all about you, and still likes you.

Elbert Hubbard

Wishing to be friends is quick work, but friendship is a slow ripening fruit.

Aristotle

HE HAS NO ENEMIES, BUT IS INTENSELY DISLIKED BY HIS FRIENDS.

Oscar Wilde

The only way to have a friend is to be one.

Ralph Waldo Emerson

Yes'm, old friends is always best, 'less you can catch a new one that's fit to make an old one out of.

Sarah Orne Jewett

Rare as is true love, true friendship is rarer.

Jean de La Fontaine

Lovers have a right to betray you... friends don't.

Judy Holliday

Time is too slow for those who wait, too swift for those who fear, too long for those who grieve, too short for those who rejoice, but for those who love, time is eternity.

Henry Van Dyke

FRIENDSHIP MULTIPLIES THE GOOD OF LIFE AND DIVIDES THE EVIL.

Baltasar Gracian

Since there is nothing so well worth having as friends, never lose a chance to make them.

Francesco Guicciardini

Instead of loving your enemies – treat your friends a little better.

Edward W. Howe

The real test of friendship is: can you literally do nothing with the other person? Can you enjoy those moments of life that are utterly simple?

Eugene Kennedy

The bird a nest, the spider a web, man friendship.

William Blake

Friendship is certainly the finest balm for the pangs of disappointed love.

Jane Austen

It is important to our friends to believe that we are unreservedly frank with them, and important to friendship that we are not.

Mignon McLaughlin

Many a person has held close, throughout their entire lives, two friends that always remained strange to one another, because one of them attracted by virtue of similarity, the other by difference.

Emil Ludwig

Without wearing any mask we are conscious of, we have a special face for each friend.

Oliver Wendell Holmes

LOVE DEMANDS INFINITELY LESS THAN FRIENDSHIP.

George Jean Nathan

Never have a companion that casts you in the shade.

Baltasar Gracian

Mighty proud I am that I am able to have a spare bed for my friends.

Samuel Pepys

Life has no blessing like a prudent friend.

Euripides

Our friends interpret the world and ourselves to us, if we take them tenderly and truly.

Amos Bronson Alcott

NOTHING SO FORTIFIES A FRIENDSHIP AS A BELIEF ON THE PART OF ONE FRIEND THAT HE IS SUPERIOR TO THE OTHER.

Honoré de Balzac

THERE IS NOTHING ON THIS EARTH MORE TO BE PRIZED THAN TRUE FRIENDSHIP.

Thomas Aquinas

THE GREAT OUTDOORS

He is richest who is content with the least, for content is the wealth of nature.

Socrates

A bird doesn't sing because it has an answer, it sings because it has a song.

Lou Holtz

In the depth of winter
I finally learned that
there was in me an
invincible summer.

Albert Camus

**Forget not that the earth delights
to feel your bare feet and the
winds long to play with your hair.**

Kahlil Gibran

I still get wildly enthusiastic about little things...
I play with leaves. I skip down the street and
run against the wind.

Leo Buscaglia

EARTH LAUGHS IN FLOWERS.

Ralph Waldo Emerson

Rest is not idleness, and to lie sometimes on the grass under trees on a summer's day, listening to the murmur of the water, or watching the clouds float across the sky, is by no means a waste of time.

John Lubbock

Spring is nature's way of saying, "Let's party!"

Robin Williams

Green is the prime colour of the world, and that from which its loveliness arises.

Pedro Calderon de la Barca

Come forth into the light of things, let nature be your teacher.

William Wordsworth

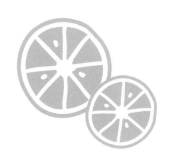

I go to nature to be soothed and healed, and to have my senses put in order.

John Burroughs

Flowers are the sweetest things God ever made and forgot to put a soul into.

Henry Ward Beecher

FOR IN THE TRUE NATURE OF THINGS, IF WE RIGHTLY CONSIDER, EVERY GREEN TREE IS FAR MORE GLORIOUS THAN IF IT WERE MADE OF GOLD AND SILVER.

Martin Luther

200

I thank you God for this most amazing day, for the leaping greenly spirits of trees, and for the blue dream of sky and for everything which is natural, which is infinite, which is yes.

e. e. cummings

In all things of nature there is something of the marvellous.

Aristotle

A light wind swept over the corn, and all nature laughed in the sunshine.

Anne Brontë

And this, our life, exempt from public haunt, finds tongues in trees, books in the running brooks, sermons in stones, and good in everything.

William Shakespeare

Just living is not enough... one must have sunshine, freedom, and a little flower.

Hans Christian Andersen

All my life I have tried to pluck a thistle and plant a flower wherever the flower would grow in thought and mind.

Abraham Lincoln

Wherever you go, no matter what the weather, always bring your own sunshine.

Anthony J. D'Angelo

Birds sing after a storm; why shouldn't people feel as free to delight in whatever remains to them?

Rose Kennedy

Keep your face to the sunshine and you cannot see a shadow.

Helen Keller

Sunshine is delicious, rain is refreshing, wind braces us up, snow is exhilarating; there is really no such thing as bad weather, only different kinds of good weather.

John Ruskin

AUTUMN IS A SECOND SPRING WHEN EVERY LEAF IS A FLOWER.

Albert Camus

The butterfly counts not months but moments, and has time enough.

Rabindranath Tagore

The sun, with all those planets revolving around it and dependent on it, can still ripen a bunch of grapes as if it had nothing else in the universe to do.

Galileo Galilei

ADOPT THE PACE OF NATURE: HER SECRET IS PATIENCE.

Ralph Waldo Emerson

I was drinking in the surroundings: air so crisp you could snap it with your fingers and greens in every lush shade imaginable offset by autumnal flashes of red and yellow.

Wendy Delsol

A good roast of sun, it slows you, lets you relax – and out here if there's anything wrong, you can see it coming with bags of time to do what's next. This is the place and the weather for peace, for the cultivation of a friendly mind.

A. L. Kennedy

I never knew I liked to be outside so much. I never knew I liked lochs and views and that, but I could seriously handle living in a cottage by the side of somewhere like this.

Jenn Fagan

We both loved the birds and animals and plants. We both felt far happier out of doors. I felt a peace in nature that I could never find in the human world, as you know.

Tracy Rees

Where lies your landmark, seamark, or soul's star?

Gerard Manley Hopkins

. . . so wondrous wild, the whole might seem the scenery of a fairy dream.

Walter Scott

THE STARS WERE BETTER COMPANY ANYWAY. THEY WERE VERY BEAUTIFUL, AND THEY ALMOST NEVER SNORED.

David Eddings

I am extremely happy walking
on the downs... I like to have
space to spread my mind out in.

Virginia Woolf

Think while walking,
walk while thinking,
and let writing be but
the light pause, as the
body on a walk rests in
contemplation of wide
open spaces.

Frédéric Gros

And into the forest I go, to lose my mind and find my soul.

John Muir

He stood there a moment, listened to the creek, and let the mountain air blow against his face. Even with all this heartache, it was beautiful here.

Eowyn Ivey

Go for a walk outdoors. Reconnect with the feeling of the wind blowing through your hair. Listen to the birds that live in a tree in your yard. Watch the sunset. Take time to smell the flowers that bloom in the park during the summer. The natural world is just as natural as it ever was, except there's less of it than there was twenty-five years ago – and most of us don't make a point of enjoying it often enough.

Skye Alexander

Be healthy by being outdoors in the natural daylight with nature!

Steven Magee

When I asked Father Tom where we find God in this present darkness, he said that God is in creation, and to get outdoors as much as you can.

Anne Lamott

My tent doesn't look like much but, as an estate agent might say, 'It is air-conditioned and has exceptional location.'

Fennel Hudson

I NEVER SAW A DISCONTENTED TREE. THEY GRIP THE GROUND AS THOUGH THEY LIKED IT, AND THOUGH FAST ROOTED THEY TRAVEL ABOUT AS FAR AS WE DO.

John Muir

You lift your head, you're on your way, but really just to be walking, to be out of doors. That's it, that's all, and you're there. *Outdoors is our element: the exact sensation of living there.*

Frédéric Gros

I stand holding the apple in both hands. It feels precious, like a heavy treasure. I lift it up and smell it. It has such an odour of outdoors on it I want to cry.

Margaret Atwood

Let the rain kiss you. Let the rain beat upon your head with silver liquid drops. Let the rain sing you a lullaby.

Langston Hughes

Earth and sky, woods and fields, lakes and rivers, the mountain and the sea, are excellent schoolmasters, and teach some of us more than we can ever learn from books.

John Lubbock

The mountains are calling and I must go.

John Muir

By reading the scriptures I am so renewed that all nature seems renewed around me and with me. The sky seems to be a pure, a cooler blue, the trees a deeper green. The whole world is charged with the glory of God and I feel fire and music under my feet.

Thomas Merton

I BELIEVE IN GOD, ONLY I SPELL IT NATURE.

Frank Lloyd Wright

When nature has work to be done, she creates a genius to do it.

Ralph Waldo Emerson

GIVE ME ODOROUS AT SUNRISE A GARDEN OF BEAUTIFUL FLOWERS WHERE I CAN WALK UNDISTURBED.

Walt Whitman

There are always flowers for those who want to see them.

Henri Matisse

Let us learn to appreciate there will be times when the trees will be bare, and look forward to the time when we may pick the fruit.

Anton Chekhov

To sit in the shade on a fine day and look upon verdure is the most perfect refreshment.

Jane Austen

A woodland in full color is awesome as a forest fire, in magnitude at least, but a single tree is like a dancing tongue of flame to warm the heart.

Hal Borland

Nature will bear the closest inspection. She invites us to lay our eye level with her smallest leaf, and take an insect view of its plain.

Henry David Thoreau

If one way be better than another, that you may be sure is nature's way.

Aristotle

Forests, lakes, and rivers, clouds and winds, stars and flowers, stupendous glaciers and crystal snowflakes – every form of animate or inanimate existence, leaves its impress upon the soul of man.

Orison Swett Marden

Trees are the earth's endless effort to speak to the listening heaven.

Rabindranath Tagore

YOSEMITE VALLEY, TO ME, IS ALWAYS A SUNRISE, A GLITTER OF GREEN AND GOLDEN WONDER IN A VAST EDIFICE OF STONE AND SPACE.

Ansel Adams

One touch of nature makes the whole world kin.

William Shakespeare

Nature teaches more than she preaches. There are no sermons in stones. It is easier to get a spark out of a stone than a moral.

John Burroughs

I remember a hundred lovely lakes, and recall the fragrant breath of pine and fir and cedar and poplar trees. The trail has strung upon it, as upon a thread of silk, opalescent dawns and saffron sunsets.

Hamlin Garland

EVERY FLOWER IS A SOUL BLOSSOMING IN NATURE.

Gerard De Nerval

ONE MUST ASK CHILDREN AND BIRDS HOW CHERRIES AND STRAWBERRIES TASTE.

Johann Wolfgang von Goethe

I think that I shall never see a poem lovely as a tree.

Joyce Kilmer

LET A HUNDRED FLOWERS BLOOM, LET A HUNDRED SCHOOLS OF THOUGHT CONTEND.

Mao Tse-Tung

The poetry of the earth is never dead.

John Keats

My recollection of a hundred lovely lakes has given me blessed release from care and worry and the troubled thinking of our modern day. It has been a return to the primitive and the peaceful.

Hamlin Garland

Breathless, we flung us on a windy hill, laughed in the sun, and kissed the lovely grass.

Rupert Brooke

The sea is everything. It covers seven tenths of the terrestrial globe. Its breath is pure and healthy. It is an immense desert, where man is never lonely, for he feels life stirring on all sides.

Jules Verne

NATURE ALWAYS WEARS THE COLORS OF THE SPIRIT.

Ralph Waldo Emerson

Never measure the height of a mountain until you have reached the top. Then you will see how low it was.

Dag Hammarskjold

It is not so much for its beauty that the forest makes a claim upon men's hearts, as for that subtle something, that quality of air that emanates from old trees, that so wonderfully changes and renews a weary spirit.

Robert Louis Stevenson

The flower is the poetry of reproduction. It is an example of the eternal seductiveness of life.

Jean Giraudoux

TO ME A LUSH CARPET OF PINE NEEDLES OR SPONGY GRASS IS MORE WELCOME THAN THE MOST LUXURIOUS PERSIAN RUG.

Helen Keller

Perhaps the truth depends on a walk around the lake.

Wallace Stevens

For every person who has ever lived there has come, at last, a spring he will never see. Glory then in the springs that are yours.

Pam Brown

The ground we walk on, the plants and creatures, the clouds above constantly dissolving into new formations - each gift of nature possessing its own radiant energy, bound together by cosmic harmony.

Ruth Bernhard

Nothing is so beautiful as
spring - when weeds, in wheels,
shoot long and lovely and lush;
thrush's eggs look little low
heavens, and thrush through
the echoing timber does so rinse
and wring the ear, it strikes like
lightning to hear him sing

Gerard Manley Hopkins

I believe that if one always looked at the skies, one would end up with wings.

Gustave Flaubert

Let the gentle bush dig its root deep and spread upward to split the boulder.

Carl Sandburg

It is only in the country that we can get to know a person or a book.

Cyril Connolly

LIKE MUSIC AND ART, LOVE OF NATURE IS A COMMON LANGUAGE THAT CAN TRANSCEND POLITICAL OR SOCIAL BOUNDARIES.

Jimmy Carter

I knew, of course, that trees and plants had roots, stems, bark, branches and foliage that reached up toward the light. But I was coming to realize that the real magician was light itself.

Edward Steichen

To be interested in the changing seasons is a happier state of mind than to be hopelessly in love with spring.

George Santayana

People from a planet without flowers would think we must be mad with joy the whole time to have such things about us.

Iris Murdoch

Nothing is more memorable than a smell. One scent can be unexpected, momentary and fleeting, yet conjure up a childhood summer beside a lake in the mountains.

Diane Ackerman

How strange that nature does not knock, and yet does not intrude!

Emily Dickinson

THERE IS A MUSCULAR ENERGY IN SUNLIGHT CORRESPONDING TO THE SPIRITUAL ENERGY OF WIND.

Annie Dillard

What makes a river so restful to people is that it doesn't have any doubt – it is sure to get where it is going, and it doesn't want to go anywhere else.

Hal Boyle

Life has loveliness to sell, all beautiful and splendid things, blue waves whitened on a cliff, soaring fire that sways and sings, and children's faces looking up, holding wonder like a cup.

Sara Teasdale

DEEP IN THEIR ROOTS, ALL FLOWERS KEEP THE LIGHT.

Theodore Roethke

Nature knows no pause in progress and development, and attaches her curse on all inaction.

Johann Wolfgang von Goethe

We do not see nature with our eyes, but with our understandings and our hearts.

William Hazlitt

Each blade of grass has its spot on earth whence it draws its life, its strength; and so is man rooted to the land from which he draws his faith together with his life.

Joseph Conrad

Nature's peace will flow into you as sunshine flows into trees. The winds will blow their own freshness into you, and the storms their energy, while cares will drop off like autumn leaves.

John Muir

Nature is so powerful, so strong. Capturing its essence is not easy – your work becomes a dance with light and the weather. It takes you to a place within yourself.

Annie Leibovitz

I DECIDED THAT IF I COULD PAINT THAT FLOWER IN A HUGE SCALE, YOU COULD NOT IGNORE ITS BEAUTY.

Georgia O'Keeffe

To cherish what remains of the Earth and to foster its renewal is our only legitimate hope of survival.

Wendell Berry

I perhaps owe having become a painter to flowers.

Claude Monet

Hope is the only bee that makes honey without flowers.

Robert Green Ingersoll

There is nothing in which the birds differ more from man than the way in which they can build and yet leave a landscape as it was before.

Robert Wilson Lynd

I am not bound for
any public place, but
for ground of my own
where I have planted
vines and orchard
trees, and in the heat
of the day climbed
up into the healing
shadow of the woods.

Wendell Berry

The groves were God's first temples.

William C. Bryant

The snow itself is lonely or, if you prefer, self-sufficient. There is no other time when the whole world seems composed of one thing and one thing only.

Joseph Wood Krutch

Love thou the rose, yet leave it on its stem.

Edward G. Bulwer-Lytton

Those little nimble musicians of the air, that warble forth their curious ditties, with which nature hath furnished them to the shame of art.

Izaak Walton

THE LAKE AND THE MOUNTAINS HAVE BECOME MY LANDSCAPE, MY REAL WORLD.

Georges Simenon

LOOK DEEP INTO NATURE, AND THEN YOU WILL UNDERSTAND EVERYTHING BETTER.

Albert Einstein

FAMILY MATTERS

Family is not an important thing – it's everything.

Michael J. Fox

Family means no one gets left behind or forgotten.

David Ogden Stiers

The love of family and the admiration of friends is much more important than wealth and privilege.

Charles Kuralt

Cherish your human connections – your relationships with friends and family.

Barbara Bush

Spend some time this weekend on home improvement; improve your attitude toward your family.

Bo Bennett

THE FAMILY IS THE NUCLEUS OF CIVILIZATION.

Will Durant

There is no doubt that it is around the family and the home that all the greatest virtues, the most dominating virtues of human, are created, strengthened and maintained.

Winston S. Churchill

My family is my strength and my weakness.

Aishwarya Rai

A HAPPY FAMILY IS BUT AN EARLIER HEAVEN.

George Bernard Shaw

A family can develop only with a loving woman as its centre.

Karl Wilhelm Friedrich Schlegel

I believe the world is one big family, and we need to help each other.

Jet Li

THE FAMILY IS ONE OF NATURE'S MASTERPIECES.

George Santayana

A man should never neglect
his family for business.

Walt Disney

You have to defend your honor. And your family.

Suzanne Vega

Family is the most
important thing in
the world.

Princess Diana

THERE'S NOTHING I VALUE MORE THAN THE CLOSENESS OF FRIENDS AND FAMILY, A SMILE AS I PASS SOMEONE ON THE STREET.

Willie Stargell

SHOW ME A FAMILY OF READERS, AND I WILL SHOW YOU THE PEOPLE WHO MOVE THE WORLD.

Napoléon Bonaparte

This is part of what a family is about, not just love. It's knowing that your family will be there watching out for you. Nothing else will give you that. Not money. Not fame. Not work.

Mitch Albom

You can kiss your family and friends goodbye and put miles between you, but at the same time you carry them with you in your heart, your mind, your stomach, because you do not just live in a world but a world lives in you.

Frederick Buechner

I sustain myself with the love of family.

Maya Angelou

A dog reflects the family life. Whoever saw a frisky dog in a gloomy family, or a sad dog in a happy one? Snarling people have snarling dogs, dangerous people have dangerous ones.

Arthur Conan Doyle

I HAVE LEARNED THAT TO BE WITH THOSE I LIKE IS ENOUGH.

Walt Whitman

Strangers are just family you have yet to come to know.

Mitch Albom

You need to make time for your family no matter what happens in your life.

Matthew Quick

Family isn't blood. It's the people who love you. The people who have your back.

Cassandra Clare

Sticking with your family is what *makes* it a family.

Mitch Albom

While we try to teach our children all about life, our children teach us what life is all about.

Angela Schwindt

When I walk, I walk
with you. Where I go,
you're with me always.

Alice Hoffman

We must take care of our families
wherever we find them.

Elizabeth Gilbert

Travelling in the company of those we love is home in motion.

Leigh Hunt

You are born into your family and your family is born into you. No returns. No exchanges.

Elizabeth Berg

Is this what family is like: the feeling that everyone's connected, that with one piece missing, the whole thing's broken?

Trenton Lee Stewart

The way you help heal the world is you start with your own family.

Mother Teresa

So much of what is best in us is bound up in our love of family, that it remains the measure of our stability because it measures our sense of loyalty.

Haniel Long

Mother is a verb. It's something you do. Not just who you are.

Cheryl Lacey Donovan

275

GOD IS THE DESIGNER OF THE FAMILY.

Gordon B. Hinckley

If you live in each other's pockets long enough, you're related.

Jodi Picoult

WE ARE NOT DEFINED BY THE FAMILY INTO WHICH WE ARE BORN, BUT THE ONE WE CHOOSE AND CREATE. WE ARE NOT BORN, WE BECOME.

Tori Spelling

If a country is to be corruption free and become a nation of beautiful minds, I strongly feel there are three key societal members who can make a difference. They are the father, the mother and the teacher.

Abdul Kalam

I'll never stop dreaming that one day we can be a real family, together, all of us laughing and talking, loving and understanding, not looking at the past but only to the future.

LaToya Jackson

For me, nothing has ever taken precedence over being a mother and having a family and a home.

Jessica Lange

The family is the first essential cell of human society.

Pope John XXIII

Women's natural role is to be a pillar of the family.

Grace Kelly

As the family goes, so goes the nation and so goes the whole world in which we live.

Pope John Paul II

All of us grow up in particular realities – a home, family, a clan, a small town, a neighborhood. Depending upon how we're brought up, we are either deeply aware of the particular reading of reality into which we are born, or we are peripherally aware of it.

Chaim Potok

Dignity is not negotiable. Dignity is the honour of the family.

Vartan

I was born into the most remarkable and eccentric family I could possibly have hoped for.

Maureen O'Hara

WITHOUT A FAMILY, MAN, ALONE IN THE WORLD, TREMBLES WITH THE COLD.

André Maurois

The greatest thing in family life is to take a hint when a hint is intended - and not to take a hint when a hint isn't intended.

Robert Frost

The bond that links your true family is not one of blood, but of respect and joy in each other's life.

Richard Bach

I come from that society and there is a common thread, specifically family values – the idea that you do anything for your family, and the unconditional love for one's children.

Ednita Nazario

My family comes first.
Maybe that's what
makes me different
from other guys.

Bobby Darin

When trouble comes, it's your
family that supports you.

Guy Lafleur

A family is a place where principles are
hammered and honed on the anvil of
everyday living.

Charles R. Swindoll

I grew up in a big family with a lot of kids around, and I definitely want to have children as well.

Heidi Klum

I am the baby in the family, and I always will be. I am actually very happy to have that position. But I still get teased. I don't mind that.

Janet Jackson

If one is desperate for love, I suggest looking at one's friends and family and see if love is all around. If not, get a new set of friends, a new family.

Jasmine Guy

If we abandon marriage, we abandon the family.

Michael Enzi

TO US, FAMILY MEANS PUTTING YOUR ARMS AROUND EACH OTHER AND BEING THERE.

Barbara Bush

Both within the family and without, our sisters hold up our mirrors: our images of who we are and of who we can dare to be.

Elizabeth Fishel

My father used to play with my brother and me in the yard. Mother would come out and say, "You're tearing up the grass"; "We're not raising grass," Dad would reply. "We're raising boys."

Harmon Killebrew

I have a family to support. And I'm not always going to be doing exactly what I want to do.

Patrick Warburton

I am the family face; flesh perishes, I live on.

Thomas Hardy

AS A GENERAL THING, WHEN A WOMAN WEARS THE PANTS IN A FAMILY, SHE HAS A GOOD RIGHT TO THEM.

Josh Billings

I mean, I look at my dad. He was twenty when he started having a family, and he was always the coolest dad. He did everything for his kids, and he never made us feel like he was pressured. I know that it must be a great feeling to be a guy like that.

Adam Sandler

I've given it my all. I've done my best. Now, I'm ready with my family to begin the next phase of our lives.

Richard M. Daley

Happy is said to be the family which can eat onions together. They are, for the time being, separate, from the world, and have a harmony of aspiration.

Charles Dudley Warner

ONE OF THE THINGS THAT BINDS US AS A FAMILY IS A SHARED SENSE OF HUMOUR.

Ralph Fiennes

MY FAMILY IS MORE IMPORTANT THAN MY PARTY.

Zell Miller

I consider my mom and all my sisters my friends.

Alexa Vega

Pray in your family daily, that yours may be in the number of the families who call upon God.

Christopher Love

MY FAMILY WAS MY GUIDE TO MY REALITY.

Haywood Nelson

I REALIZED MY FAMILY WAS FUNNY, BECAUSE NOBODY EVER WANTED TO LEAVE OUR HOUSE.

Anthony Anderson

A woman can plan when to have her family and how to support a family.

Kathleen Turner

Also, my mom and family are very important to me and I know that this is not expected.

Christina Milian

I've always put my family first and that's just the way it is.

Jamie Lee Curtis

I love my family.

Manute Bol

I never did quite fit the glamor mode. It is life with my husband and family that is my high now.

Patty Duke

I THINK TOGETHERNESS IS A VERY IMPORTANT INGREDIENT TO FAMILY LIFE.

Barbara Bush

The family you come from isn't as important as the family you're going to have.

Ring Lardner

Give a little love to a child, and you get a great deal back.

John Ruskin

I love cooking for myself and cooking for my family.

Al Roker

It takes a lot of work to put together a marriage, to put together a family and a home.

Elizabeth Edwards

One's family is the most important thing in life. I look at it this way: one of these days I'll be over in a hospital somewhere with four walls around me. And the only people who'll be with me will be my family.

Robert Byrd

WHEN I REMEMBER MY FAMILY, I ALWAYS REMEMBER THEIR BACKS. THEY WERE ALWAYS INDIGNANTLY LEAVING PLACES.

John Cheever

Family, nature and health all go together.

Olivia Newton-John

Dad kept us out of school, but school comes and goes. Family is forever.

Charlie Sheen

WHEN YOU START ABOUT FAMILY, ABOUT LINEAGE AND ANCESTRY, YOU ARE TALKING ABOUT EVERY PERSON ON EARTH.

Alex Haley

I would rather start a family than finish one.

Don Marquis

Tennis is just a game, family is forever.

Serena Williams

The joke in our family is that we can cry reading the phone book.

Ron Reagan

The one thing that kept our family together was the music. The only thing that our family would share emotionally was to have our dad cry over something the kids did with music.

Dennis Wilson

Make a Goal Box, a chart of positive daily contact with a family when you are working with them.

Richard G. Scott

I HAVE THESE VISIONS OF MYSELF BEING THIRTY, THIRTY-FIVE, FORTY HAVING A FAMILY.

Nastassja Kinski

WE LOVE TO BE WITH OUR FAMILY AND FRIENDS AND I CAN TELL YOU THAT LOTS OF EATING WILL BE INVOLVED.

Julia Barr

When I'm ready, I plan to adopt. I still believe in family.

LaToya Jackson

We went to church every Sunday. When I was a kid, the only time I sang was around my family.

Darius Rucker

SOME OF THE MOST IMPORTANT CONVERSATIONS I'VE EVER HAD OCCURRED AT MY FAMILY'S DINNER TABLE.

Bob Ehrlich

I have a lot of very close girlfriends and sisters
- I'm from an all female family. My father
often quips that even the cat was neutered!

Shirley Manson

I find the family the most mysterious and fascinating institution in the world.

Amos Oz

I grew up in a very religious family. I could read the Qur'an easily at the age of five.

Akhmad Kadyrov

I LIVE QUIETLY AT HOME AMONG MY FAMILY AND FRIENDS.

Antonio Tabucchi

We'll sort of get over the marriage
first and then maybe look at the kids.
But obviously we want a family so
we'll have to start thinking about that.

Prince William

THE FOUNDATION OF FAMILY - THAT'S WHERE IT ALL BEGINS FOR ME.

Faith Hill

MY FAMILY BACKGROUND WAS DEEPLY CHRISTIAN.

Abbé Pierre

For all of those willing to help me start a family, I am flattered. I will let you know when I need your help.

Paula Abdul

My life comes down to three moments: the death of my father, meeting my husband, and the birth of my daughter. Everything I did previous to that just doesn't seem to add up to very much.

Gwyneth Paltrow

When I was younger, my family would go camping and fishing on our ranches. My dad loves being around all kinds of animals. He's the one who got me to be a really big animal lover.

Paris Hilton

Little children are still the symbol of the eternal marriage between love and duty.

George Eliot

I stay in tune with my family and God.

Regina King

You leave home to seek your fortune and, when you get it, you go home and share it with your family.

Anita Baker

In every conceivable manner, the family is the link to our past, the bridge to our future.

Alex Haley

I don't know if I believe in marriage. I believe in family, love and children.

Penelope Cruz

Peace is the beauty of life. It is sunshine. It is the smile of a child, the love of a mother, the joy of a father, the togetherness of a family. It is the advancement of man, the victory of a just cause, the triumph of truth.

Menachem Begin

If you cannot get rid of the family skeleton, you may as well make it dance.

George Bernard Shaw

THE ONLY ROCK I KNOW THAT STAYS STEADY, THE ONLY INSTITUTION I KNOW THAT WORKS, IS THE FAMILY.

Lee Iacocca